# Skytrain to Nowhere

**Brandon Adamson**

**Briny Books**
Phoenix, AZ 85032

Copyright © 2018 Brandon Adamson

All rights reserved. This book or any portion thereof may not be reproduced or used in any manner whatsoever without the express written permission of the publisher except for the use of brief quotations in a book review or scholarly journal.

First Printing: 2018

ISBN 978-0-692-12462-8

www.briny.org

Dedicated to my mother

# SKYTRAIN TO NOWHERE

# SECRET OF THE SKYTRAIN

The secret of the skytrain
is that it never stops moving for too long.
It thrives on agility, mobility, progression while only
occasionally reaching into the messenger bag
of the past to refresh from old notes
and retrace steps along familiar routes of your favorite maps

To remain in motion is to drink the potion of life,
like an emerging transhuman with vampirist ambitions,
new, youthful blood must be transfused frequently
in the form of a steady stream of riders, maintainers
and well funded appreciators.

Observe the action,
The clockwork commotion
the here and there
the back and forth
the comings and goings
now departing... now arriving...
next stop Terminal 4... next stop Terminal 3...
Please stand clear of the doors and
allow passengers to exit

Just as a river must constantly flow to remain clean,
free from pollution and toxic waste,
the skytrain impregnates the tunnel with the seed of vitality
each time it arrives and leaves...
but never sticks around long enough for the relationship to stagnate
If Sky Harbor International airport was
converted into a self-contained city, and
there were no planes, no airline passengers, and
no constant stream of visitors,
would the energy still be there?
Only if its inhabitants found a way to
always keep moving and
within their own veins
discovered the secret of the skytrain.

A POSTCARD TO THE SUN

The skytrain climbs the incline of the rail like
a Wally World roller coaster making it's initial ascent
up the track,
as the rider begins to anticipate and brace himself
for the inevitable downward spiral on the other side
of the hill...

but from this angle the skytrain's path seems
headed straight through the clear blue skies,
on a path past the goddess Venus
with her sulfuric acid clouds and floating cities
until finally reaching the messenger god Mercury
who couriers us on like a mailman with a vacation postcard,
directly into the sun.
I throw on a pair of my best Gucci pilot sunglasses
cause I know Icarus did nothing wrong.

Just then the skytrain reaches the other end of the hill and
uneventfully descends back down toward the Earth.

SKY TALKERS

There's no music
just a
mid pitched hum
transformed by the vibrations of the skytrain
against the track
into a barely detectable beat
vaguely resembling Morse code beeps.
The other passengers don't seem to notice it,
only me.
If only I still had my trusty Fisher Price
Sky Talker Walkie Talkies
from 1983.
They had a chart in the form of a sticker
that could be used to decode any potential,
even incidental message.
Instead I'm stuck having to sit here, wonder and
pretend it says...

"ALL THESE WORLDS ARE YOURS EXCEPT EUROPA"

## SKYTRAIN STOWAWAY

"Not on my watch, skytrain!"
an annoying young man of genetically Mestizo origins
loudly and obnoxiously proclaims in a faux-ebonic dialect
as he slips in through the door at
the last possible moment
just before the train is about to leave.
Without missing a beat, he immediately proceeds to
hoot and holler and make as much
noise as inconsiderately possible.

Oh great

I wanted to keep this positive
with a meditative focus on
the skytrain as
a state of the art, awe-inspiring piece of machinery
representing a technological milestone in
what mankind can potentially achieve.

I promise, this time..
The last thing I intended was to turn this optimistic,
uplifting experience into
tales of a cynic griping
about loud and obnoxious minorities
on public transit.

Blocking out the annoying young man's behavior to the extent an
overactive imagination is enough to turn a blind eye...
still can't help but wonder,
if this train is headed for the future,
is he the stowaway
or am I?

## SAFETY CARD

Standing room only this time
the skytrain is packed like
a jar of pimento olives
sure
feels like we're floating all right
when I look out the window
can't even see the side of the tracks.
It suddenly seems as though I'm on
the equivalent of a poor man's amusement park thrill ride
you know
like a dilapidated escalator in a third world country
or an elevator that hasn't been serviced in a while.
For the first time
a sense of danger and an irrational fear
a realization of the potential for derailment
as I visualize the skytrain plunging toward
the unforgiving asphalt below
with me in it.

survival instinct contingent
kicks in
my eyes strategically, yet frantically
glancing around
nothing to grab onto but a pole that
looks more like it was made for dancing
and strippers...It's
a pole
positioned poorly for survival in this instance,
and it makes me a tad anxious
to be unprepared,
minus a worst case scenario mental safety pamphlet with
ready bake tactics and
instructions on what to do in case one needs to
brace for possible impact,

but we're still floating
for now...

as the apparent necessity of the skytrain's functionality
becomes more intertwined with my own sense of mere mortality,
my investment in it deepens proportionally

PORTRAIT OF A SKYTRAIN

Pale concrete and shades of metallic gray feature heavily
in the aesthetic of the skytrain,
owing to the steel, aluminum and other alloys
which compose of the vehicle's construction.
The colors and materials are
those of a clean, lightweight, no-nonsense,
aerodynamically designed machine.
Silver, translucence and gray
the marks of modern efficiency
on display in the 21st century desert city of
New Phoenix.
Unlike the gaudy, bulky, blocky monstrosities of
a once promising age ,
the skytrain was built for simple function and agility
without the need for exotic or pretentious excess.
Featuring subtle accents of yellow and occasional
signs of illuminated green, the skytrain is a visually
moving work of transit technology.

## THE WILDERNESS AFAR

Finally I'd catch a break
if I were young enough to notice and not be taken to task
and still had enough
time to regret letting such opportunities pass me by
in that long since sealed off tunnel of
teenage turmoil...
when I was only slightly less immature and obnoxious, but
uncomfortably more awkward, lazy, abrasive and shy...
as for once today,
instead of the dregs of a Pepperidge Farm
goldfish cracker bag
the train is filled with an
entire high school aged girls basketball team,
the Wyoming Beasts, with each member wearing a blue t-shirt featuring
the Tigresian eyes of their beastly mascot.

The skytrain whizzes by some cacti
or cactuses
sparsely situated on the white concrete barrier slope.
A beast speaks, remarking that "cacti is the plural of cactus..."
which it is, (but apparently so is cactuses)
The word cacti is repeated seven or eight times,
but after the second or third she begins to pronounce it
"cock-tie" while sporting a Baby-Sitters Club tier mischievous grin.
Still, the whole lot of these precocious girls is less noisy than
the Somali lady who was shouting inconsiderately into
her cellphone on a previous journey.
It's quiet enough to think, and my mind has
already moved on to other things beyond the beast within,
it's focused now on the beast we're riding in
and where it could head someday but won't be going today.

What if the skytrain traveled all the way to Wyoming?
Think of the wildlife, the creatures we'd see on the ride:
bobcats, wolves, black bears, frolicking all along the rail line,

maybe even a porcupine!

Even better if the train could take us there but
arrive in another time, perhaps when Clint Eastwood was
filming Every Which Way But Loose in 1977 or 1978.
Jackson, Wyoming
We could hang with Philo Beddoe and Clyde the orangutan
and stick around for Any Which Way You Can
in 1980.

It's all I can think of...
Wyoming Cowboys
college football team
had cool uniforms in the 80's
and unlike most teams, still do.
Flashback
Holiday Bowl
1987
They lost a close game, but what a great team from
a great place.

An automated female's recorded voice can almost be heard emanating from the skytrain's intercom
"Now departing for Jackson Wyoming...
Now arriving....
Please stand clear of the doors."

THE CANALS MUST FLOW

Peering out the window
the parking lot is filled with golf carts
hundreds of them as far
as my cycloptic eye can see.
I pretend they're moon buggies
or maybe Martian rovers
or trikes and quads from the game Dune II,
"Reporting | Acknowledged | Yes, sir! | Movin' Out|"
   since the Phoenix desert
   looks absolutely nothing like the moon,
the surface aesthetic more closely resembling that of Dig Dug levels...
with shades of beige, sienna, burnt umber and mahogany.

The mountains assert themselves from far off in the distance
as the skytrain jets around a corner dutifully,
and we come across of all things,
a canal.

The canals of Mars
will one day be built and flow,
becoming another of man's achievements in plain view for
skytrain passengers to overlook and take for granted
on their morning commute.

BUBBLE GIRL

Young girl | early 20's
steps onto the skytrain
a few extra pounds,
but it doesn't make a bit of difference
beautiful blue eyes | auburn hair | pale skin
NAU sweatshirt and tight black leggings.
She's chewing a lemon yellow piece of bubble gum,
possibly banana flavored
chewing with her mouth wide open, but
for once it doesn't bother me
doesn't trigger my misophonic rage
as I shoplift a couple of glimpses of her and
abort when I notice she's sporting a wedding / engagement ring.

Why are all these young millennial girls engaged or
married all of the sudden?
Traditionalism is awakening like the undead?
peering out from a shallow grave and
rearing its ugly head? Ha
yeah right,
more like
      the wedding industrial complex strikes again.

Every time I glance over at her, she's staring at me.
Our eyes lock for an unusually long time.
Feeling the desire to lose a staring contest / crack the ice, I acknowledge her with a token, barely detectable "hi,"
spoken under my breath.

With her bubble gum still clearly visible, as inviting to my eyes as a vintage Slip 'N Slide on a summer's day in 1985,
she mouths the word...

"Hi."

setting in motion once again
the familiar sensation of premature nostalgia.

It was innocent, though I would have impregnated her in an instant if circumstances permitted, but they didn't. They couldn't?
As she got off the skytrain she took one last look back at me
and I made a quick scan,
Travelers Club luggage and Michael Kors handbag.
I already knew we had nothing much in common,
and she was wearing a wedding ring.
The outcome was predetermined by contextual calculation.
The creepy candy corn connection was

|     all in my head,     |
| and... I have a girlfriend! |

What a waste of time, energy and space to be thinking about this, but I have to admit that I did.

SKYTRAIN FEVER

The speckled finish of the floor of
the pedestrian bridge leading to the skytrain
sparkles like a Kustom tuck-and-roll covered amplifier.
Laminated glass panels emit hues of blue and amber ambiance from
the walls,
subtly illuminating the otherwise dimly lit corridor.
It's mood lighting
fit for trip to a 25th century disco.

This majestic skyway serves as a preliminary segue to
       the skytrain which can take
us to that place in our minds where
one small corner of the world is briefly transformed into
a private light up dance floor,
where we can be free to strut our stuff.

Charlie's Angels, Leisure Suit Larry,
       Buck Rogers, Laura, Miss Cosmos and Dr. Theopolis...
They're all going to be there,

ready to get down.

THE ALTERNATE PAYLINE

Not even the skytrain knows it yet,
but this one's now departing
not for Terminal 4
now departing
for
Las Vegas
please stand clear of the doors
this train is now departing
vultures circling
297 miles of southwest landscape matte paintings
and a Mojave desert later
now arriving at McCarran airport

born to be alive!

stop off at The Flamingo
admire the wildlife
chat with a parrot
automated chair massage
play a game of Money Mad Martians slots
25 cents Max 3 credits
flying saucer
Bonus
"155!"

Next up, King Cash
25 cents
Max 3 credits
3 lion heads
Bonus
"Here we go!
   first offer
 40
final offer
   200
Yeah!"

Cash out and dash
wander for days and/or
hop on the skytrain
head for home
now departing... now arriving...
or maybe I could just stay and
never come back..
monorail?
tram
brass railing
moving walkway
Excalibur
Sword and the Stone Bar
just one
a few
another day

PARALLELONOIA

This train is out of service
another will be here in 5 minutes
This train is out of service
an unexpected disruption of
minor inconvenience
the next train arrives,
but now it appears
everything is subtly out of sync
like the door slid open
into a parallel universe
or a duplicate planet
something's a bit off
just a tad different
the skytrain that normally comes
from the opposing direction, now
passes by at a slightly different time and place.
It had always occurred at
the same exact moment
don't think anyone else notices
but like Roy Thinnes and Vera Miles I'm
on the lookout for near mirror images,
doppelgangers from the far side of the sun

THE OASIS

Even without a drop of water
A skytrain in the desert is
an oasis all its own
a sanctuary in motion which briefly insulates
from the unforgiving elements
of mundane and untamed humanity
set to a backdrop which takes on the appearance of
harmless mountains in the distance.

A skytrain in the desert is
an oasis all its own.
The mirages are those images you see when you
gaze outside:
cardboard cutouts of the machineries
of advanced civilizations
especially the people and places
once you reach destinations
upon closer examination
there's nothing more to them.

## NAUTICAL DREAMER

Such a cool cerulean blue
is the all enveloping sky
as the skytrain cruises smoothly along.
If one turns on imagination and doesn't look down
it almost feels like...
we're
   underwater,
traveling through a transparent, aquarius tunnel
along the shallow seabed
tepidly peering out the window for signs of marine wildlife
a lone thrasher bird morphs into Ecco the Dolphin and
swims right up to the glass to sing
a playful song
as unwary pedestrians outside transmute into
octopuses, mako sharks,
starfish, kelp, sea turtles and alluring,
scantily clad
Aryan mermaids invitingly frolicking about among
the ancient artifacts and occasional Diet Pepsi bottles which
litter the briny ocean floor.

Flashback to being on the Submarine Voyage
ride at Disneyland in 1986,
the captain's voice narration can be heard over the loudspeaker:
"these classic ruins could very well be the remains of
the lost continent of Atlantis."

I can't help but wonder if Atlantis had a skytrain or
would have had one sometime,
long before now
had the island not been buried in ash,
tastelessly destroyed by an epic eruption of volcanic marmalade.
I want to ride the skytrain with New Atlanteans
through vast technological cities and
make love to animatronic mermaids.

TREADMILL TO NEONOPOLIS

A retro futuristic city,
straight out of 3-D WorldRunner
World 8
with its exotic towers of translucent turquoise,
bright white cylindrical condominiums,
and communal recreational facilities of fluorescent peach,
looms in the distance,
it's visibility partially obscured by
a thin layer of smog
a stubbornly lingering residue
of a transitional yet primitive polluting era,
a barrier which stands between us and the "sanctuarian" Neonopolis.

The sky train approaches and approaches
but can never seem to get much closer,
like a teenager ineffectually running down an endless hallway
in a horror movie cliche or stumbling around a
fun house at the fair and other illusory optical obstacles.
We are peons on a treadmill facing a hologram of the neon city,
which through belief alone we cannot reach

## THE BRIGHTNESS

One thing that consistently stands out in
the daytime skytrain experience is

the brightness!

not quite the searing sensation felt by a vampire who
forgot his Ray-Ban sunglasses while
watching the sunrise one morning
but more like that of a 20th century man
waking up from a 500 year cryonic sleep
and getting a glimpse of the future he was promised
for the first time.

The brightness overwhelms the senses and
energizes the spirit of anyone who enters the skytrain
with transitional dreams for mankind or
is conscious enough to appreciate a
brief escape from their own dreary lives.

## SKYTRAIN : THE FRAGRANCE

Unlike the subway and light rail systems,
which frequently reek of piss and
retain a sweaty odor of
unkempt subhuman beasts,
the skytrain always adorns the aroma of
a brand new set of designer luggage
straight off the rack from TJ Maxx,

It's as if there's a new car scented,
Little Trees air freshener
being dangled from the hand of
an invisible, mechanical elf above

but it's just human workers doing
a thorough job
they may or may not love

SKYTRAIN BRAINGAMES

I wonder whether you're more likely to
die in a derailment of a skytrain

a passenger plane crash

a shark attack

or be bitten by a frightened bat, like the one
that's flying erratically overhead
within the walls of the main concourse of Terminal 4,
trapped,
echo-locating its escape from a world it does not recognize

## MUSICAL EAMES CHAIRS

Even when it's nearly empty,
seats are scarce
on the skytrain,
with just four in total...
made of sleek, minimalist and sterile plastic.
Sitting on them is about as inviting to the derrière as
a game of mid-century modern musical Eames chairs in
the late afternoon of a blowoff day in class
and as comfortable as reading in the seating area of
a 1980's laundromat
while waiting for your clothes to dry.

a feature not a bug
They're not designed for relaxation like
the debit card operated massage chairs
but to keep you on your toes,
for brief journeys and short bursts of speed

The skytrain is always on the go
Don't make yourself feel too at home.

# THE PILOT AND THE FLIGHT ATTENDANT

Bless you
   Thank you I'm so glad you realized
   it was a sneeze...
   most people think I have a cough,
   but it's a sneeze
Where you headed?
   Lubbock
I'm working tonight. Then I'm headed to Philly.
   It's weird that they're
   getting so much snow this time of year
   and Chicago
   in April!
           Baseball!
 It's so crazy
 so crazy

IN BETWEEN SKYTRAINS

In between skytrains,
I find myself idle
with a few minutes in the station,
surrounded by strangers whom I can either creepily observe,
eavesdrop on their casual conversations, or
just tune out their frequencies
and let my thoughts swerve...

Unless there's an attractive girl,
I almost always choose number 3.
Even then I take care to restrict my actions to my own private world,
mostly just pace back and forth and
ponder age old questions the world may never know the answers to like

>"How many licks does it take to
>get to the Tootsie Roll center of a Tootsie Pop?"

Well, how much productive ground can really
be covered in a 4 minute daydream?

The mind races with a heightened sense of urgency and anticipation,
a million miles of nonsense if
my thoughts were stretched out on a roll of film
to be parsed through and analyzed in a lab of psychologists
or an assembly of the finest New Atlantean astrologers.

In the background,
pre-recorded voices issue commands relating to
escalator safety and protocol
   "Please avoid the sides of the escalator"
   "...push carts and pull carts are not allowed on the escalator"
   "Hope you enjoy riding this escalator. Have a nice day."
The repetitive statements function as a hypnotic form of
verbal muzak.
The spoken word escalator music has a calming effect,
until the next skytrain arrives and
lifts me out of the trance.

## 48 SECONDS

Spotted in the wild
my bearded, black male, afro-futurist counterpart
seated across from me on the skytrain
jotting things down in his composition notebook
writing who knows what
he looks forward out the window
like me
mostly keeping to himself
wrapped up in an self-serious session of mental masturbation
while others engage in even more pointless
cross talk and
superficial conversation

We ride the skytrain like two unlikely,
reluctant partners
in an 80's buddy cop movie...

all the way to the box office or at least
the VHS clearance rack at one of the few remaining
Suncoast locations.

## THE UNFATHOMED

Fat security man stares for an uncomfortably long time,
his peepers peer from the upper outline of his dwarven figure and
glare through sunglasses like the black eyes of
a juvenile great white shark that might be mistaking me for lunch.

Bathing in suspicion,
he no doubt wonders why I'm always riding the skytrain
with no apparent destination, and
he reflexively assumes the worst
like typical bored mall cops
he's another security guard on a power trip
probably thinks
I'm a skytrain flight risk
maybe even a homegrown terrorist.

Someone like him could probably not fathom
that anyone might simply
have a profound appreciation for this glorious machine
and would enjoy riding it for its own sake
as a meditative, recreational activity, occasionally
treating themselves to the majestic,
panoramic view of an entire city.

In all the thousands of hours he has spent here
I wonder if he has ever even seen it.

## STOICS OF THE DESERT

How odd it must be for the elder creatures of the desert:
Gila monsters, chuckwallas and horned lizards.
to watch the skytrain zoom by.
Do they perceive it as a possible predator,
something that's alive, like
a giant silver pterodactyl, soaring through the prehistoric sky?
Maybe they view it as another harmless extension of the Earth's
ever changing environment, and
stoically observe as humans manipulate it like Play-doh
into increasingly unfamiliar formations

LIMITED CONNECTIVITY

Spotted a red piece of luggage that
oddly resembled an unfinished game of Connect 4,
with a grid of columns of
yellow dots
   arranged
 in
a
   pattern

that didn't quite connect to victory

Not a metaphor,
just literally a man's luggage that looked like
a game of Connect 4

## THE SILVER INGOT

The skytrain sparkles,
dazzles and
wows, glistening as it reflects
the mid-day sun,
piquing our interest like a shiny silver ingot
old west outlaws left in
the middle of the desert for
us to someday find.

a time capsule,
an inheritance,
a building block.

MIRAGE-O-RAMA

"Watch your children when they're near the pool,"
reads the billboard.
Another features a picture of a large cruise ship in the ocean
and says, "Power Cruise!"
which quickly dissolves like a Saved By the Bell dream sequence into
oh wait
turns out it's just an ad for the Powerball lotto
before cross fading into yet another
advertisement,
this one for the Lost Lake Festival

The skytrain sails through the middle of a desert drenched in
Neptunian illusions

## THOUGHTS ON THE RAMPAGE

The skytrain exits the terminal
like a slow motion silver bullet
leaving the barrel of a cybernetic pistoleer's gun...
focused, determined and
heading straight for the heart of a giant werewolf
who's rampaging throughout the city.

It's a routine microcosmic battle for civilization that's
repeated every few minutes like clockwork.
The skytrain is efficient, methodical and
single minded in proceeding toward its destination,
as New Atlantean enthusiasts wage a two front battle...
against the havoc which unintended mutational creations of
their experiments unleash and

against the primitivists who'd prefer we raze all buildings and
return to simple existence as
mice in the fields
subject to the whims of the plow.

LET IT GO

A rather energetic and agile man in his late 30s
practically dives through the door as it's closing in
order to make the train.

He succeeds.

I brace for him to be obnoxious and rowdy, since
there is something inherently annoying about someone who so stubbornly
feels the need to prove they can make a particular train when

these skytrains arrive and depart every 3-5 minutes

high time preference
      lack of patience
       a misplaced sense of urgency

No it has to be this train

"I can almost reach it..."

After making his needlessly dramatic entrance
he amusingly remarked that it was like Indiana Jones.

I laughed at that.
Suddenly I could relate
and ended up being wrong about him anyway
He said nothing else,
just "Whew, Indiana Jones."

nothing much after that

I had an Indiana Jones and the Temple of Doom lunchbox
when I was a kid, which
is still in my closet sitting there
like an artifact waiting to be dug up

# THE ELDER DWELLERS

Fossilized eyes,
belonging to Freeway off-ramp art in the form of a creature,
appear to peer back at the skytrain and say
"hey I remember when this desert was all mine."

Flashback to an obscure childhood memory in the mid 1980's
when terminal 4 was still under construction,
and the interior resembled more of a Home Depot
than the colossal, state of the art transportation hub that
the skytrain now runs through
hundreds of times per day.
I recall my uncle pointing up at the exposed support beams
and enthusiastically explaining what it was that was being built.

I revisit this memory and the those associated with it
with every trip.

So many places, faces in the city I barely recognize

My own fossilizing eyes
appear to peer out from the skytrain and say
"hey I remember when this desert was all mine..."

and that's why I still stick around for the rides.

IN THE LOOP

Hands with faded maroon nail polish on fingernails
holding a fire engine themed lunch kit
belonging to a thin and personable, light brown haired woman whose
only beauty crime was to have spent a few too many years in the sunlight

"This is my first time riding this...
the skytrain,"
she says to her male companions.

One of them, while making a motion with his hand,
jokingly tries to convince her that the skytrain loops upside down like a roller coaster.

She's not buying it all. Meanwhile,
I have a vision of Roy Scheider looping a chopper in Blue Thunder

# BROCHURES

"Please face forward while riding this escalator,"
the recorded female voice commands,
decent advice maybe,
but I'm too nostalgic for that
have to occasionally glance back and
check to make sure my favorite daemons
are still with me.

I don't mind them hanging around, as
long as they're down to keep moving
in one form or another
don't want to get bogged down.

They have mapped out part of the maze already
could come in handy if
I reach another dead end

Time isn't a river

BRANCHING OUT

If I were a skytrain I would probably zig zag a lot
mostly forward and aiming to progress
further ahead
but navigating the tracks of time like an eager child
traces the broken branches of a tree,
in place of drawing fixed shapes and
straight lines.

THE HABITUATED

As time goes on,
I'm less interested in the passengers
hardly noticing them now,
even the most obnoxious subhumans and salacious beauties
only evoke a token glare or glance.
Their conversations reduced to low frequency radio static...
A fluorescent vested beast, noisily suckling on her water bottle
and smacking her lips
barely registers on the needle.

I feel like a once-green soldier that's adapted to the jungle marshes
and can move among the native inhabitants without detection,
partially immersed in the elements and
a molecularly rearranged participant in my own half-witted
Philadelphia experiment.

My senses totally fixated on what's ahead,
anticipating the glimpse of
the skytrain which approaches from the opposite direction.
We're just a couple of vaguely trapezoidal prisms
meeting again like veteran old friends
for a game of shuffleboard.

REVISITING TOMORROWLAND

A billboard in passing
"Win tickets to Disneyland"
double take

"Win tickets to Disneyland"

Never really thought about it, but
riding the monorail
and the PeopleMover
at Disneyland in the summer of 1986
may have been the ignition switch that sparked my interest or
enduring childlike fascination
with futuristic modes of transportation, such as the skytrain.

I've never been back since that trip with my grandparents.
I waited too long,
most of my favorite rides and attractions
replaced and irretrievably gone, like taped over VHS and Betamax tapes.
the people too, have passed on...
and it's expensive now
so there's no point.

Maybe, the skytrain is my ticket back to the Disneyland
that I've lost,
and each casual commute opens a portal through
tomorrowland, yesteryear,
and today.

THE POP-UP SKYTRAIN

Does the skytrain's location self-select for cleanliness
and low-key civility?
acting as a filtration for riders
that can't afford airline tickets

and those ripoff resort fees?

If the skytrain ran through the middle of the city
and was still free, would it still retain the look and feel of state of the art technology? or would it swiftly degenerate into just another traveling gallery of micro-horrors,
in the name of representing humanity?

SKY-TRANSAMERICA

A postmeridian skytrain ride on
a sparsely clouded Phoenician day
carves out a 3D experiential replication of a kid
coasting toward the backdrop of
a desert level in Rad Racer on
a summer vacation afternoon in 1989...

so much time to live

parents won't be home for hours

the vehicles for anxiety, dread and apprehension trail at their slowest speeds,
temporarily occupying
their weakest positions on the mind's highway

THE FEEDBACK

A sign says
"How's your ride?
Send us your Skytrain feedback."

All I can think of is that the skytrain
could use some flirtatious animatronic stewardesses...

and maybe a couple of back issues of SkyMall magazine
so that riders can peruse pages of inflatable travel pillows,
adjustable massage footrests and
Skel-E-Gnome garden statues.

Implementing these suggestions
would enhance the experience

SKYTRAIN TO NOWHERE

Sometimes it's worthwhile to
take in the view from the skytrain exactly as it appears.
Look through the window and see nothing but
liquid blue skies that turn to layers of orange, lavender, and
magenta against the setting sun,
culminating in the most colorful display of
track lighting one could ask for from this world...

    (or even another if it's on a night like March 13, 1997,)

the surrounding mountainous regions tinted by a light haze and
swirls of distant, fevered desert dust,
buildings from an amalgam of architectural styles:
        mid-century modern, ranch, Tuscan, Spanish hacienda, art deco,
        from old west to
        21st century new suburbanist,
            self-contained subdivisions

and miles upon miles of surviving 1980's strip malls, 7-11s and Circle K's

but still reserving enough tracts of open spaces to offer
        more than a few places to hide buried treasure
among the evidence of
a contemporary city partially in motion outside
within the immediate valley of the sun.

Even if the skytrain doesn't yet physically venture anywhere beyond
Terminal 2
  Terminal 3
    Terminal 4
  The East Economy Station
  and 44th St Metro Rail,
there's still room for enough adventure and beauty to go around,
even without activating one's imagination or feeling much
inspiration for any particular vision of
the past, present, or
  alternating futures

Remember that all skytrain riders are micro-time travelers,
as time passes more slowly
for those that keep moving
(quickly,)
and they'll soon be living at
least a fraction of a second further into the future and
one step ahead of stagnant outsiders who remain stationary,
within newly distinct, chronological classes.
If simple courtesy isn't enough, count that as one more reason
not to be an annoyingly slow walker.

"Explore the Moment" reads the caption of
a recently erected billboard, now visible from the skytrain.

Enticing would-be travelers to visit the state of Montana, it features
a man and a woman rowing a small boat through a calm lake,
with snowy peaked, commanding mountain ranges in the background.

Not exactly my idea of a dream destination, but
fresh injections of riders with whims of their own,
are waiting in Icarus' wings,

and the electronic voice of an unknown goddess issues an open-ended challenge to those who enter her domain:

"Prepare to board the skytrain to nowhere
and go there, or
please stand clear of the doors
and allow passengers to exit."

## ABOUT THE AUTHOR

Named after the main character in a sleazy 1970's romance novel (*The Flame and the Flower*,) Brandon Adamson is a writer who currently resides in Phoenix, Arizona. He has been writing since 1995, and his work has appeared in many magazines, blogs and literary journals over the years.

www.ingramcontent.com/pod-product-compliance
Lightning Source LLC
Chambersburg PA
CBHW031417040426
42444CB00005B/613